EXPOSING
THE JTF2 SNIPER
RECORD

AF372470

EXPLORE THE INTRICACIES OF THE LONGEST SNIPER SHOT IN COMBAT HISTORY, DELVING INTO THE TECHNICAL CHALLENGES, EQUIPMENT, AND TACTICS.

by KALEL TAVILA

Cataloguing in Publication (CIP) - Catalogue record developed by the author

Tavila, Kalel
    Exposing the JTF2 Sniper Record / Kalel Tavila.
    NMT-RS-BR: First Edition, 2024.
    46 p.

    ISBN   978-65-00-97906-0

    1. Ballistics 2. Firearm 3. Airgun
I. Title

                                        CDD: 623.5
                                        CDU: 799.5

                                              R1

EXPOSING THE JTF2 SNIPER RECORD
TABLE OF CONTENTS

EXPOSING THE JTF2 SNIPER RECORD

SETTING THE STAGE

▸ SETTING THE STAGE

In May 2017, a precision shooter, a sniper whose identity remains confidential, a member of the *Joint Task Force Two* or **JTF2**, a Canadian special forces unit, achieved the record for the longest confirmed kill shot in combat, up to that point.

EMBLEM OF THE JTF II

This unprecedented shot took place in Mosul, one of Iraq's largest cities. The target was a sniper from the Islamic terrorist group ISIS (Islamic State of Iraq and Syria), located 3540 meters or 3871 yards (~2.2 miles) away from the Canadian shooter and his spotter/observer partner.

The *JTF2* sniper, who maintained readiness in a building and successfully completed his mission, effectively thwarted an imminent terrorist attack by Daesh (Islamic State) against Iraqi security forces, as published.

This event was initially reported by *The Globe and Mail*, a more than century-old Canadian journalistic outlet, following a statement from the Canadian military and an interview with an undisclosed Canadian military personnel. Subsequently, this report was endorsed by other media outlets such as *The Washington Post, CNN, Sky News, Kurdistan 24*, among others.

EXPOSING THE JTF2 SNIPER RECORD
WEAPON

▶ WEAPON

The weapon used, as reported by the news, was a *McMillan TAC-50 (C15)*, a manually operated, rotary bolt-action anti-material rifle chambered in 50 BMG caliber. It features a 29-inch (73.7 centimeters) long barrel with a 1:15 twist rate.

The manufacturer claims that the rifle achieves half-MOA precision, meaning that with this equipment It is possible to obtain shot groups smaller than or equal to 0.5 MOA under optimal shooting conditions. This is actually a high precision rifle.

$$INCHES = MOA \times YARDS \div 95.5$$

Let's apply the above angular formula and then understand what half-MOA grouping means.

$$INCHES = 0.5 \times 100 \div 95.5 = 0.52\ INCHES$$
$$INCHES = 0.5 \times 200 \div 95.5 = 1.05\ INCHES$$
$$INCHES = 0.5 \times 1000 \div 95.5 = 5.2\ INCHES$$
$$INCHES = 0.5 \times 1760 \div 95.5 = 9.2\ INCHES$$

In other words, the manufacturer assures that the shooter could achieve groupings of 0.52 inches at 100 yards, 1.05 inches at 200 yards, 5.2 inches at 1000 yards, or even 9.2 inches at 1 mile (1760 yards). Therefore, under optimal conditions, two consistent shots may result in two points of impact (POI) up to 9.2 inches apart from each other on a target 1 mile away.

ANTI-MATERIAL RIFLE MCMILLAN TAC–50–A1–R2, CAL. 50 BMG

EXPOSING THE JTF2 SNIPER RECORD
AMMUNITION

▸ AMMUNITION

The brand and model of the ammunition used by the Canadian shooter were not disclosed. However, the official ammunition manufacturer for the Canadian armed forces at the time was *General Dynamics Ordnance and Tactical Systems*.

GD-OTS used to offer a line of specialized precision shooting ammunition known as *Sniper Elite*. For the 50 BMG caliber (12.7x99mm), they provided a 709-grain (45.9 grams) Ball projectile. However, the manufacturer did not provide any Ballistic Coefficient (BC) value, such as G1 or G7 pattern, nor did they offer field-tested ballistic trajectory data.

The only two pieces of ballistic data disclosed by *GD-OTS* regarding this ammunition model are its precision (grouping capability) and a single sample of projectile velocity. According to the manufacturer, the 709-grain Ball projectile achieves a velocity of approximately 860 m/s or 2821 fps after traveling 24 meters or 26 yards in the field. At the time, *GD-OTS* claimed it to be their most precise 50 BMG ammunition available, capable of achieving groupings smaller than or equal to 1.7 MOA for shots up to 1000 meters, 1094 yards, or approximately 0.62 miles away.

GD-OTS SNIPER ELITE 50 BMG 709GR BALL AMMUNITION

EXPOSING THE JTF2 SNIPER RECORD
AMMUNITION

Check the angular formula below for converting MOA to inches for a specific range in yards.

$$INCHES = MOA \times YARDS \div 95.5$$

Let's apply the above angular formula and then understand what 1.7 MOA grouping means.

$$INCHES = 1.7 \times 100 \div 95.5 = 1.78\ INCHES$$
$$INCHES = 1.7 \times 200 \div 95.5 = 3.56\ INCHES$$
$$INCHES = 1.7 \times 1000 \div 95.5 = 17.8\ INCHES$$
$$INCHES = 1.7 \times 1760 \div 95.5 = \text{31.3 INCHES}$$

In other words, the manufacturer assures that the shooter could achieve groupings of 1.78 inches at 100 yards, 3.56 inches at 200 yards, or even 17.8 inches at 1000 meters (1094 yards). Therefore, under optimal conditions, two consistent shots may result in two points of impact up to 17.8 inches apart from each other on a target 1000 meters away. Note, according to the manufacturer, the expected group size should increase for distances beyond 1000 meters, such as when engaging targets at 1 mile (1760 yards) or greater distances.

It is common for manufacturers to limit their accuracy promises for firearms and ammunitions. The best groupings, even measured in angular units, will always be achieved at limited distances. For longer distances, the grouping capability of the firearm and ammunition combination is naturally compromised by intrinsic physical effects on the projectile in flight, such as gyroscopic precession, which may have its root cause in the manufacturing process, and/or encountering the transonic region, which can lead to significant destabilization of the projectile in flight due to sudden pressure variations on its body, among others.

▸ SIGHTING DEVICE

Despite public records concerning the caliber and firearm used for the specific shot, there is uncertainty regarding the telescopic sight used, as there is no official information about this device. However, there are two most likely models of sighting devices to compose the equipment for the occasion, each recommended by the firearm manufacturer, *McMillan*, for this type of high-precision application: the *Leupold Mark 4 16x40mm LR/T M1* and the *Schmidt & Bender 5-25×56 PMII (Police Marksman II)*. Both telescopic sight devices feature a MRAD/MIL reticle pattern.

For subsequent analyses, let us consider that the aiming device employed was the *S&B 5-25x56 PMII*, due to its higher magnification capability and current use by the Canadian special forces, up to the latest publication.

SCHMIDT & BENDER 5−25×56 PMII TELESCOPIC SIGHT

EXPOSING THE JTF2 SNIPER RECORD
ADJUSTMENT TURRETS

▸ ADJUSTMENT TURRETS

The *S&B 5-25x56 PMII* aiming device is marketed in 2 options for elevation and windage adjustment turrets: $^1/_{10}$ MRAD (0.1 MRAD/MIL) click value or $^1/_4$ MOA (0.25 MOA) click value. We will adopt the $^1/_{10}$ MRAD turret pattern for our analysis because it is the most likely model used by the shooter, as the MRAD/MIL angular measurement unit is the worldwide standard in the military for telescopic sighting devices.

According to its manufacturer, the total adjustment range for the elevation turret is 26 MRAD (260 clicks) and for the windage turret it is 12 MRAD (120 clicks), with both turrets reaching full range in 2 revolutions.

SCHMIDT & BENDER 5-25×56 PMII AIMING DEVICE WITH ADJUSTMENT TURRETS WITH $^1/_{10}$ MRAD CLICK VALUE

EXPOSING THE JTF2 SNIPER RECORD

PARALLAX ADJUSTMENT

▸ PARALLAX ADJUSTMENT

The *S&B 5-25x56 PMII* sighting device features side focus parallax adjustment (SF). The adjustment scale ranges from 10 meters (11 yards) to infinity. Although 10 meters is a short distance to shoot with a precision rifle, it is a desirable feature for any aiming device that stands out for its versatility. Even with parallax adjustment up to infinity, the last consistent and indexable indication for parallax adjustment is at 1000 meters or 0.62 miles (1094 yards). Hence, any distance exceeding this specification will further complicate the task of correcting the parallax error between the reticle and the target within the shooter's line of sight (LOS). This error, an angular one, increases exponentially with the distance to the target.

SCHMIDT & BENDER 5-25×56 PMII AIMING DEVICE WITH SIDE FOCUS PARALLAX ADJUSTABLE FROM 10 METERS UP TO INFINITY

▸ RETICLE

The mentioned aiming device, the *S&B 5-25x56 PMII*, is offered in approximately 10 distinct reticle models. The selection of one or another reticle model does not lead to errors or discrepancies in the actual event results, as the requirement for any potentially applied reticle lies in the patterns of its markings. The interval for 1 DOT or 1 FHM (full hash mark) must coincide with 1 MRAD when reticle is set to a 1:1 scale, which is a worldwide military standard.

For optimal visualization of the target by the Canadian shooter, we can adopt one of the most likely reticle models used by him, called *Mil-Dot Gen II XR*, mounted in the FFP (first focal plane) of the *S&B 5-25x56 PMII* telescopic sight.

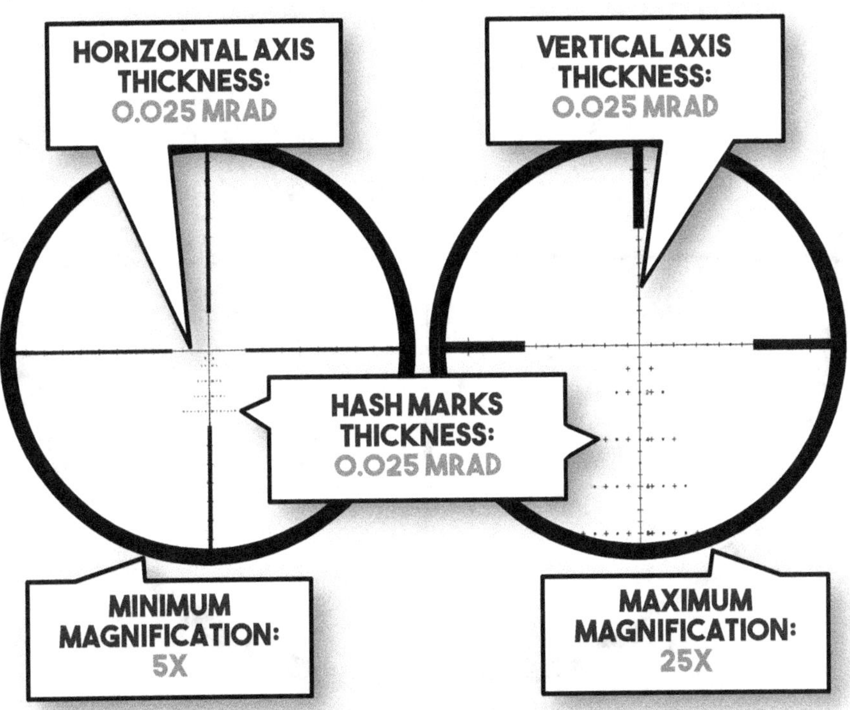

MIL-DOT GEN II XR FFP RETICLE SET AT 5X AND 25X

▸ MINIMUM MAGNIFICATION

With the *S&B 5-25x56 PMII* aiming device set to its minimum magnification of 5x, featuring *Mil-Dot Gen II XR FFP* reticle, the shooter benefits from markings extending up to 25 MRAD for shot compensations (holding over) when the target is located beyond the far zero. Within this range, enhanced precision is achieved between the reticle's center and 10 MRAD below it, in 0.5 MRAD increments. However, beyond 10 MRAD, precision notably decreases for holding over, with 2.5 MRAD increments.

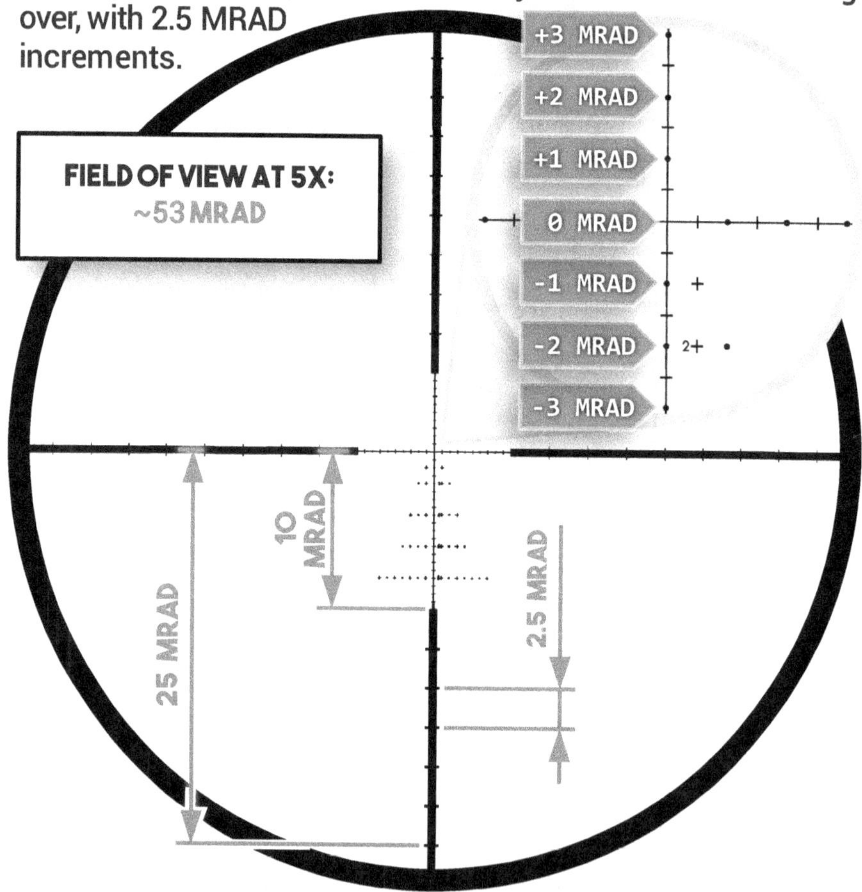

MIL–DOT GEN II XR FFP RETICLE SET AT 5X MAGNIFICATION

EXPOSING THE JTF2 SNIPER RECORD
MAXIMUM MAGNIFICATION

▶ **MAXIMUM MAGNIFICATION**

With the *S&B 5-25x56 PMII* scope set to its maximum magnification of 25x, featuring the *Mil-Dot Gen II XR* FFP reticle, the shooter benefits from markings up to 7 MRAD, in 0.5 MRAD increments, for shot compensations when the target is located beyond the far zero, enabling holdover for long-range shooting.

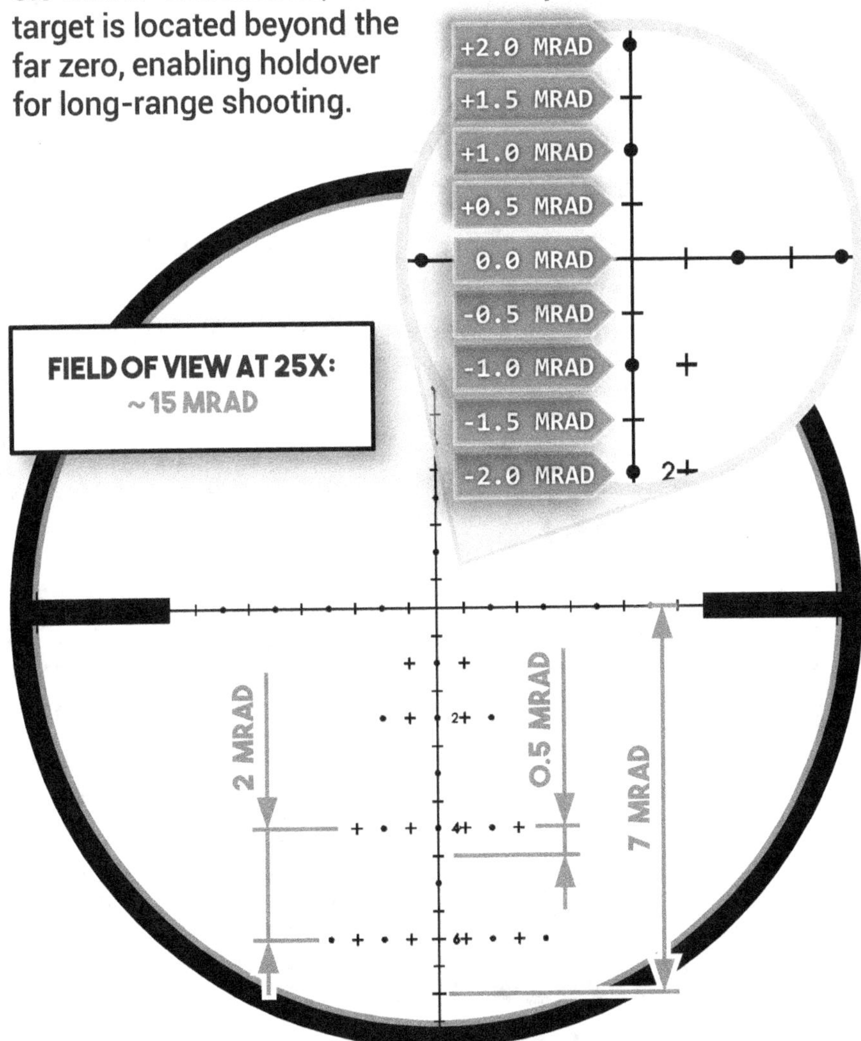

MIL-DOT GEN II XR FFP RETICLE SET AT 25X MAGNIFICATION

EXPOSING THE JTF2 SNIPER RECORD
TARGET

▶ TARGET

For the target, a sniper from the ISIS terrorist group, we will adopt the average height of an adult of the same ethnicity, therefore, 1.71 meters (~5'7") tall. Let's consider that the target was not in a prone position, common for a sniper, but standing and exposed at the moment of the shot, and located at 3540 meters or 3871 yards (~2.2 miles) away from the Canadian shooter. Let's calculate the target's height in MRAD, the standard unit of the Canadian shooter's scopes reticle.

$$OBJECT_{MRAD} = 10 \times OBJECT_{CENTIMETERS} \div DISTANCE_{METERS}$$

$$OBJECT_{MRAD} = 10 \times 171 \div 3540 = 0.483 \text{ MRAD}$$

Below is an accurately scaled illustration of the target, ~0.5 MRAD in height at 3540 meters away, as seen through the *Mil-Dot Gen II XR* FFP reticle at 25x.

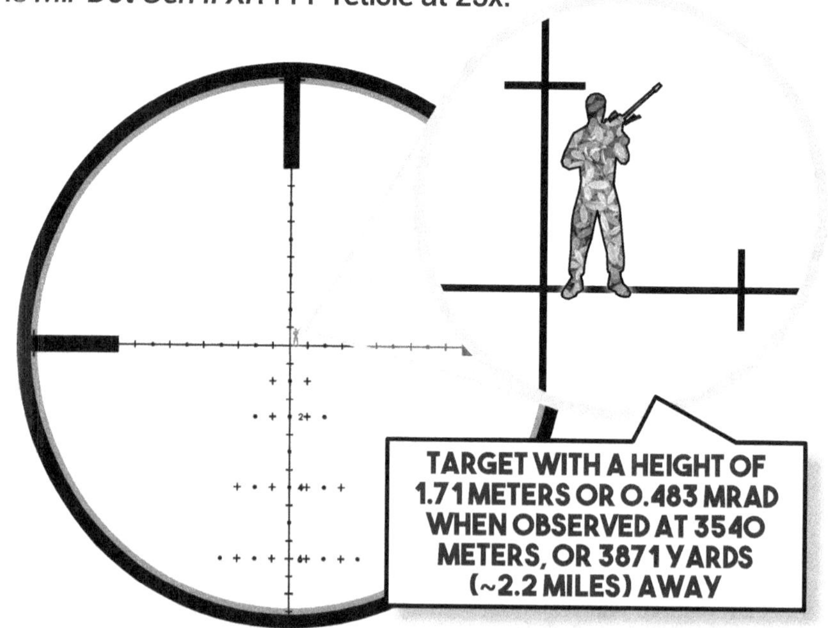

MIL-DOT GEN II XR FFP RETICLE, TARGET AT 3540 METERS, 25X

EXPOSING THE JTF2 SNIPER RECORD
KILL ZONE

▸ KILL ZONE

Let's extrapolate the target's height to presume his kill zone, the intended bullseye aimed by the shooter, considering it to be the entire chest. For a 1.71-meter (~5'7") tall target, we can consider his 13-inch or 33-centimeter wide chest as the diameter of the kill zone. We proceed to calculate the size of the target's kill zone in MRAD, which is the angular measurement unit of the reticle.

$$\text{OBJECT}_{\text{MRAD}} = 10 \times \text{OBJECT}_{\text{CENTIMETERS}} \div \text{DISTANCE}_{\text{METERS}}$$

$$\text{OBJECT}_{\text{MRAD}} = 10 \times 33 \div 3540 = 0.093 \text{ MRAD}$$

Below is an accurately scaled illustration of the target's kill zone, 0.093 MRAD in diameter at 3540 meters away, as seen through the *Mil-Dot Gen II XR* FFP reticle at 25x.

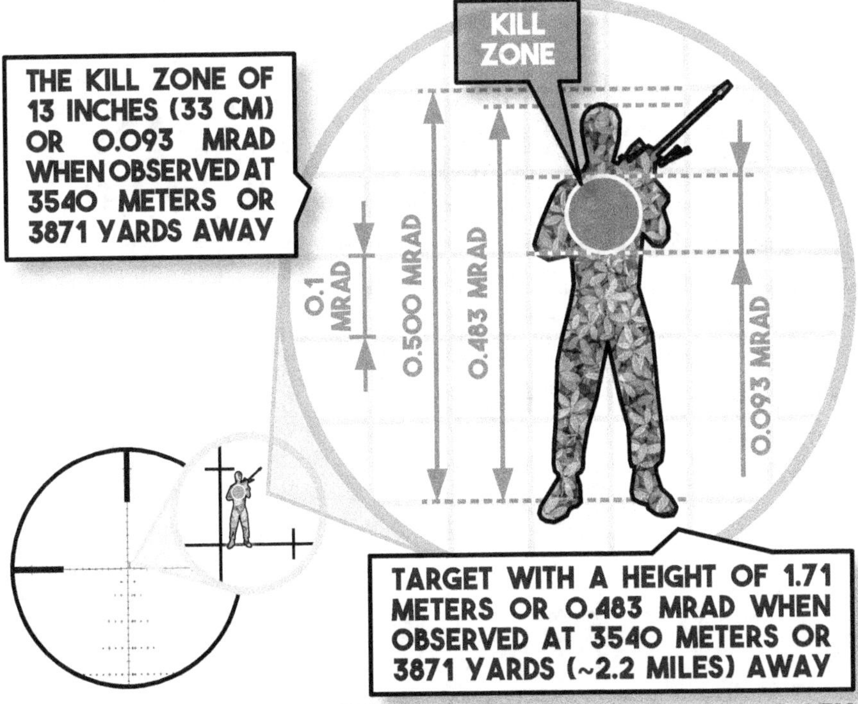

MIL–DOT GEN II XR FFP RETICLE, KILL ZONE AT 3540 METERS, 25X

▸ KILL ZONE VS. WEAPON

According to the manufacturer of the *McMillan TAC-50* rifle, the rifle is capable of achieving half-MOA precision, meaning that, under optimal conditions, two consistent shots may result in two points of impactup to 0.5 MOA apart from each other. To relate the rifle's precision to the size of the target's kill zone, we need to convert the half-MOA precision to MRAD, the angular unit of the Canadian shooter's scope reticle.

$$MRAD = MOA \div 3.44$$
$$MRAD = 0.5 \div 3.44$$
$$MRAD = 0.145\ MRAD$$

Half-MOA precision means shot groups of 0.145 MRAD or smaller. Therefore, with a kill zone of 0.093 MRAD, even under optimal conditions, the Canadian sniper could miss the target's kill zone. This is because *McMillan TAC-50* precision rifle, according to its manufacturer, can only guarantee groupings larger than the target's kill zone.

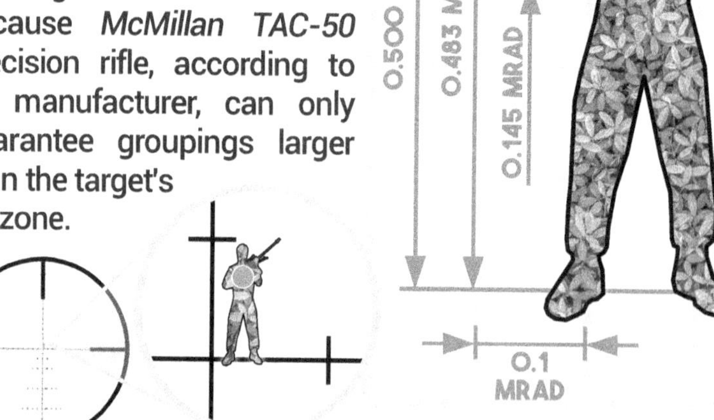

HALF-MOA RING AND KILL ZONE AT 3540 METERS, 25X

KILL ZONE VS. AMMUNITION

▸ KILL ZONE VS. AMMUNITION

According to *GD-OTS*, under optimal conditions, the *Sniper Elite 50 BMG 709 grains Ball* ammunition is capable of achieving consistent shot groups with a diameter smaller or equal to 1.7 MOA up to 1000 meters or 0.62 miles (1094 yd). To relate the ammunition precision to the size of the target's kill zone, we need to convert the 1.7 MOA precision to MRAD, the angular unit of the Canadian shooter's scope reticle.

$$MRAD = MOA \div 3.44$$

$$MRAD = 1.7 \div 3.44 = 0.494\ MRAD$$

The 1.7 MOA precision equates to shot groups of 0.494 MRAD or smaller. Thus, with a kill zone of 0.093 MRAD, even under optimal conditions, the Canadian sniper might miss the target's kill zone. This is because according to the manufacturer of the *GD-OTS Sniper Elite 50 BMG 709gr Ball* ammunition, the guaranteed groupings may be larger than the target's kill zone, or worse, the ammunition's grouping capability may exceed the size of the target itself (0.483 MIL).

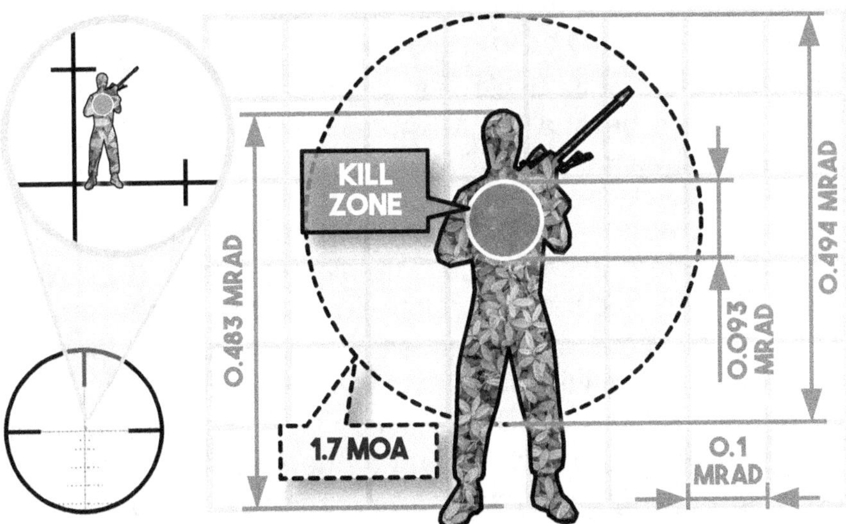

1.7 MOA RING AND KILL ZONE AT 3540 METERS, 25X

▸ KILL ZONE VS. SCOPE

The technical specifications for the *S&B 5-25x56 PMII* scope indicate a click value of 0.1 MRAD or $^1/_{10}$ MRAD. This feature might pose a challenge for the Canadian shooter because each click on the elevation or windage turret moves the reticle more than the target's kill zone diameter (0.093 MRAD).

This scenario could lead to a consistent shifting of the zero, along with ongoing adjustments via dialing or holding over. This happens because the reticle's center might never align perfectly with the firearm's precision ring (ø 0.5 MOA or 0.145 MRAD) and the ammunition's precision ring (ø 1.7 MOA or 0.494 MRAD).

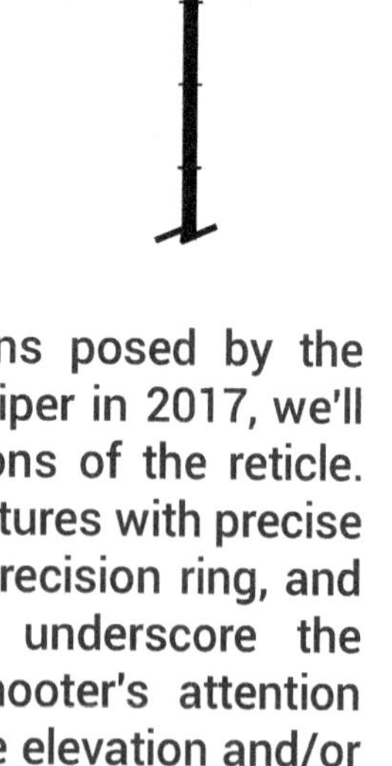

Furthermore, there's a potential concern regarding reticle subtension. The thickness of the reticle's axes and hash marks is set at 0.025 MRAD by the scope manufacturer. This thickness increases for holdovers beyond 9.5 MRAD and for wind holds beyond 5 MRAD.

To gain a better grasp of the limitations posed by the telescopic sight used by the Canadian sniper in 2017, we'll proceed with accurately scaled illustrations of the reticle. These illustrations will showcase sight pictures with precise depictions of the kill zone area, firearm precision ring, and ammunition precision ring. They will underscore the unavoidable errors that demand the shooter's attention even with a single-click adjustment on the elevation and/or windage turrets.

EXPOSING THE JTF2 SNIPER RECORD
KILL ZONE VS. SCOPE

■ Below are accurately scaled illustrations showing the points of aim (POA) displacements after just 1 click adjustments on the elevation and windage turrets. **The zero is perfectly set. It's centered with the kill zone, and the shooter cannot modify it, as shown below.**

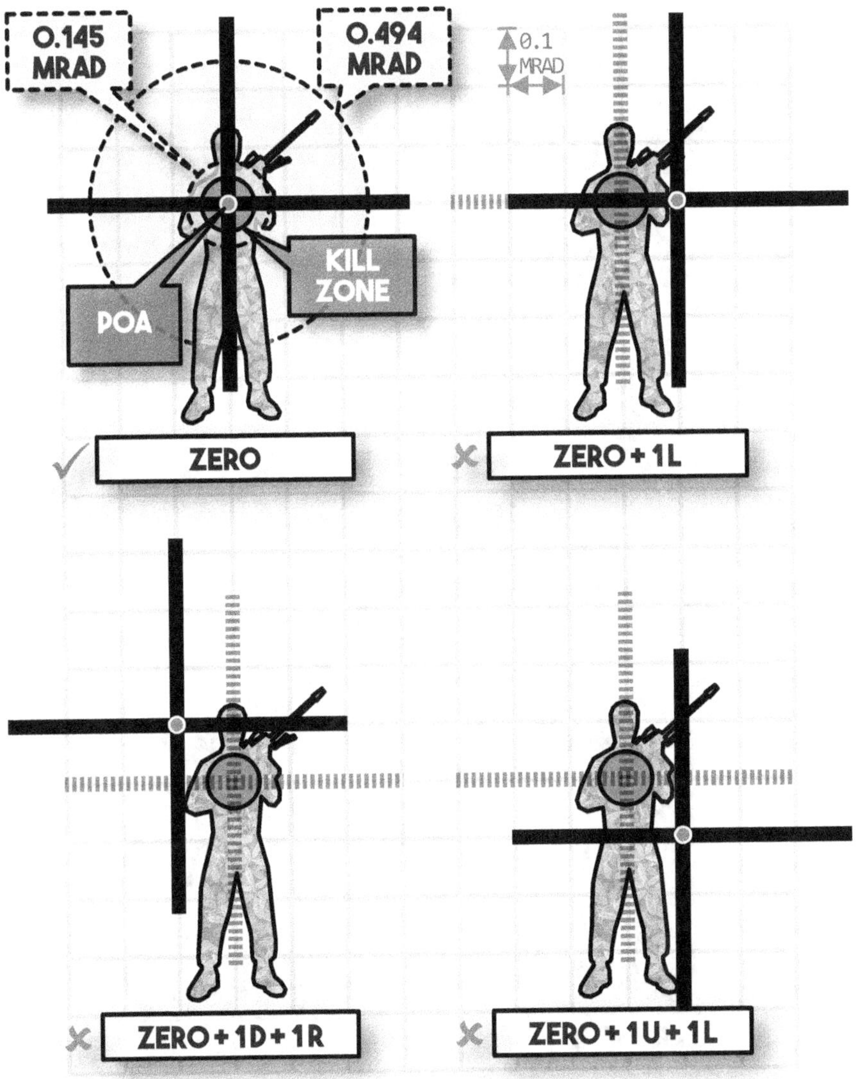

EXPOSING THE JTF2 SNIPER RECORD
KILL ZONE VS. SCOPE

▪ Below are accurately scaled illustrations showing the points of aim (POA) displacements after just 1 click adjustments on the elevation and windage turrets. **The zero is perfectly set. It's almost at the left edge of the kill zone, and the shooter cannot modify it, as shown below.**

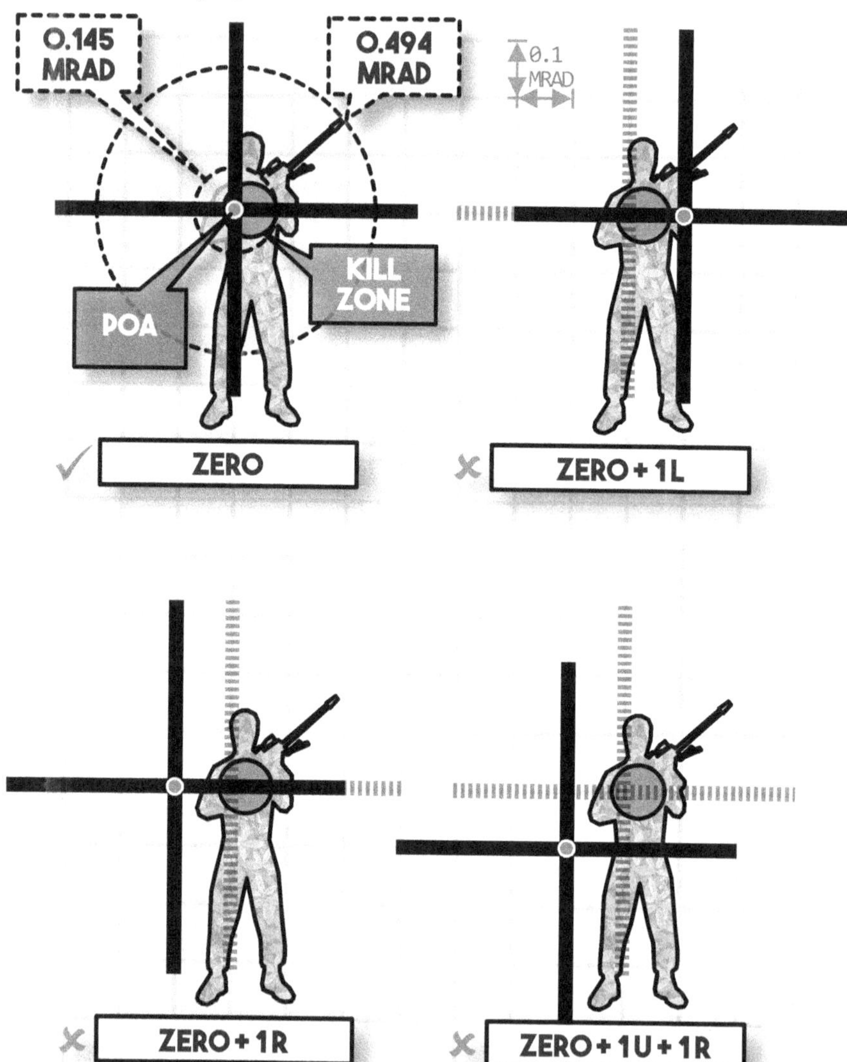

EXPOSING THE JTF2 SNIPER RECORD
KILL ZONE VS. SCOPE

■ Below are accurately scaled illustrations showing the points of aim (POA) displacements after just 1 click adjustments on the elevation and windage turrets. **The zero is perfectly set. It's almost at the upper edge of the kill zone, and the shooter cannot modify it, as shown below.**

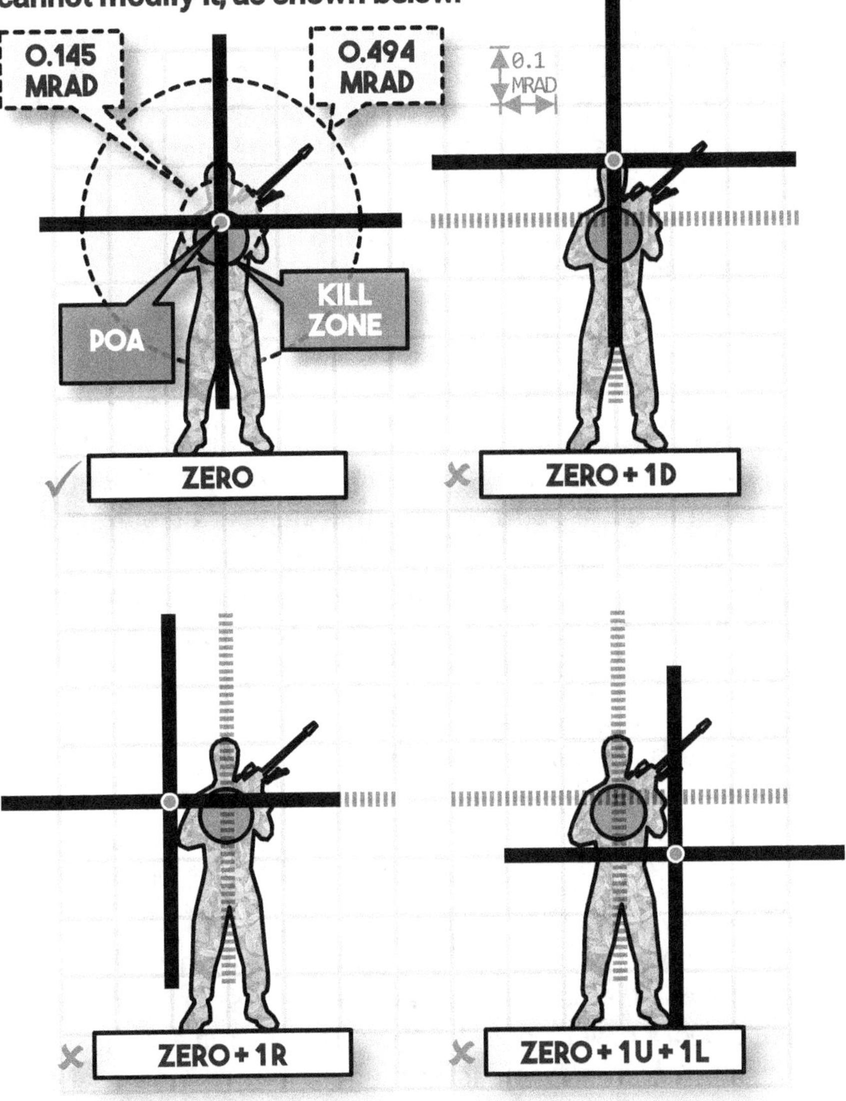

EXPOSING THE JTF2 SNIPER RECORD

ENVIRONMENT AND WEATHER

▸ ENVIRONMENT AND WEATHER

The Canadian sniper's precise shot in Mosul, Iraq, during May 2017 prompts a brief overview of the area's environmental conditions. The following data, based on typical climate patterns for May in Mosul, have been synthesized from historical registers of temperature, humidity, atmospheric pressure, and winds. While these are estimates and may vary yearly, they provide valuable insights into the sniper's environment. Here they are:

Daytime Temperature	30-38°C or 86-100°F
Nighttime Temperature	18-24°C or 64-75°F
Relative Humidity	10-30%
Barometric Pressure	29.83-29.97"Hg or 758-761 mmHg
Altitude Above Sea Level	223 meters or 732 ft
Daytime Winds	10-20 km/h or 6-12 mph (common)
Nighttime Winds	5-15 km/h or 3-9 mph (common)

To analyze the precision shot performed by the JTF2 sniper, we must speculate about environmental variables that were never disclosed. Due to the obvious relevance of the target visibility factor, we'll adopt the average daytime weather conditions for our analysis. Therefore, we have reached the environmental definition:

Temperature	34°C or 93°F
Relative Humidity	20%
Barometric Pressure	29.90"Hg or 759.5 mmHg
Altitude Above Sea Level	223 meters or 732 ft
Winds	15 km/h or 9 mph (common)

We cannot overlook the physical phenomenon of Atmospheric Refraction, common in Mosul's hot and dry weather, which can cause optical distortions, leading observers to misjudge a distant object's elevation or distance. This is crucial for a sniper and his spotter in extreme long-range shots, like the analyzed event.

EXPOSING THE JTF2 SNIPER RECORD

▸ REENACTMENT OF THE EVENT

To theoretically replicate the precise and record-breaking shot by the Canadian JTF2 sniper, we'll utilize the *Elite Ballistics* calculator app (v1.09.10). Regardless of other professional ballistic calculators, the results remain consistent due to the immutable laws of physics applied to computational calculations.

With the collected data on the sniper's scenario, we define a sight height of 4" or 10.2 cm so we can perform ballistic calculations. However, the projectile's Ballistic Coefficient (BC) is still missing and not disclosed by its manufacturer, *GD-OTS*. Nevertheless, in the ballistic calculator's database, we found a 50 BMG *Magtech* ammunition with the same projectile pattern with a BC of 0.663 G1. We still need to know the velocity of the projectile at the muzzle of the rifle, V_0. We don't have access to the firearm and ammunition set used by the Canadian sniper for any measurements, but we already have information on the projectile's velocity at 24 meters (26 yards) along its trajectory, V_{24} of 860 m/s (2821 fps). With the BC defined and all other context data, the ballistic calculator returns the V_0 of 870 m/s (2854 fps).

In general, a sniper assigned to high-value targets (HVT) as part of a special forces unit has considerable freedom in adjusting his equipment and choosing his combat location, within tactical and hierarchical parameters. This freedom extends to members of the Canadian JTF2. Given the extensive possibilities for adjusting the shooter's equipment, we'll analyze some hypotheses of zero settings for the moment the target was neutralized. Among these, we'll consider plausible zeros, such as at 500 and 1000 meters, followed by the less probable zero set to 2500 meters.

▸ HYPOTHESIS OF ZEROING SET TO 500 METERS

For the first hypothesis, let's consider the far zeroing of the sight set to 500 meters or 547 yards. Here's the ballistic table record obtained with the ballistic calculator.

Range m	Time ms	Path m	Up|Dn Click	Lt|Rt Click	Vel m/s	Energy joule
26	30	0.0↑	0	0	859	16947
500	654	0.0↓	0	7R	672	10387
3540	10K	-357↓	1K0U	73R	224	1155

BALLISTIC TABLE RECORD WITH ZERO SET TO 500 METERS

When setting the far zero at 500 meters, the near zero occurs at 26 meters (28 yards) along the projectile's trajectory. We can observe that the projectile took 10 seconds (10k ms) to reach the target, with a kinetic energy of 1155 joules (852 ft.lb).

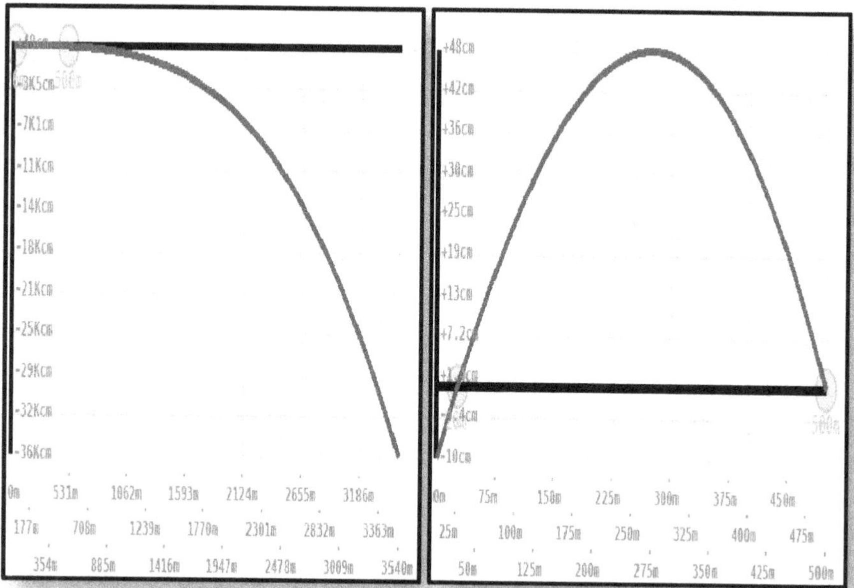

BALLISTIC CURVE WITH ZERO SET TO 500 METERS

EXPOSING THE JTF2 SNIPER RECORD
ZERO SET TO 500 METERS

Considering the anticipated crosswind for the given context, it would require 73 clicks (7.3 MRAD) in one direction on the windage adjustment turret. However, the total capacity of the *S&B 5-25x56 PMII* scope is 120 clicks (12 MRAD) with the sum of both directions, or ±60 clicks (±6 MRAD). It's worth noting that maybe wind drift correction wasn't the primary concern for the shooter at that time.

After traveling 3540 meters (3871 yards) along its trajectory, the projectile will be 357 meters (1171 ft or 14055") below the shooter's line of sight. To compensate for the projectile drop through the elevation adjustment turret, it would require 1000+ clicks (1k0 Up) or 100+ MRAD, however the scope only supports a maximum of 260 clicks or 26 MRAD, as previously seen. Nevertheless, even if the scope allowed for 1000+ clicks, if the shooter missed counting just one click (0.1 MRAD) out of a thousand resulting in a counting error of 0.1%, he would completely miss the target's kill zone, which measures 0.093 MRAD in diameter.

To compensate for the projectile drop through the shooter's line of sight, it would be necessary to position the reticle's center 100+ MRAD above the target. Thus, even at the minimum magnification (5x), which offers a 25 MRAD range for holdover, the shooter would still be unable to see his target at the moment of the shot. For the record, the projectile reaches its highest elevation at 273 meters (299 yards) along its trajectory, rising 48 centimeters or 0.48 meters (1.57 ft) above the shooter's line of sight.

Range	Time	Path	Up|Dn	Lt|Rt	Vel	Energy
m	ms	cm	Click	Click	m/s	joule
273	336	48	17D	3R	759	13217

HIGHEST ELEVATION WITH ZERO SET TO 500M

▸ HYPOTHESIS OF ZEROING SET TO 1000 METERS

For the first hypothesis, let's consider the far zeroing of the sight set to 1000 meters or 1094 yards. Here's the ballistic table record obtained with the ballistic calculator.

Range m	Time ms	Path m	Up|Dn Click	Lt|Rt Click	Vel m/s	Energy joule
11	12	0.0↑	0	0	865	17205
1000	1K5	0.0↓	0	15R	504	5837
3540	10K	-337↓	953U	73R	224	1154

BALLISTIC TABLE RECORD WITH ZERO SET TO 1000 METERS

When setting the far zero at 1000 meters, the near zero occurs at 11 meters (12 yards) along the projectile's trajectory. We can observe that the projectile took 10 seconds (10k ms) to reach the target, with a kinetic energy of 1154 joules (851 ft.lb).

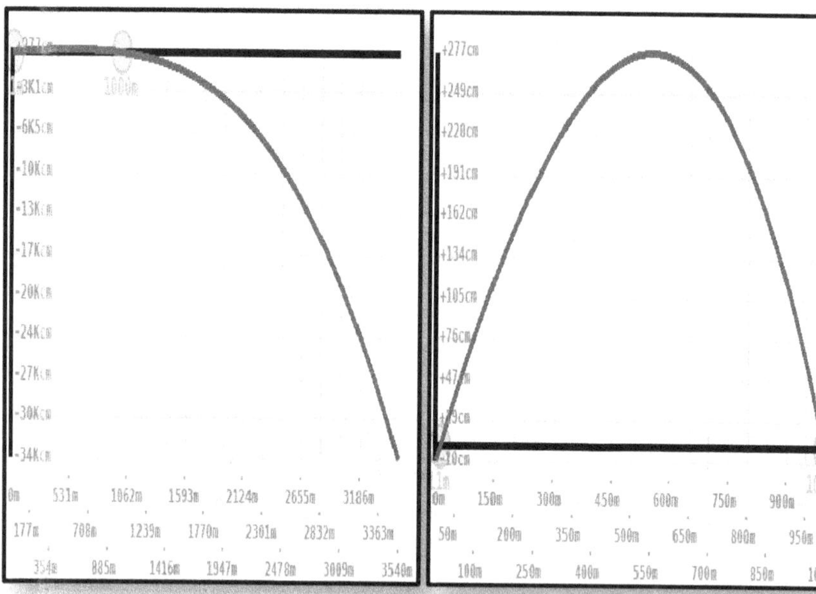

BALLISTIC CURVE WITH ZERO SET TO 1000 METERS

Considering the anticipated crosswind for the given context, it would require 73 clicks (7.3 MRAD) in one direction on the windage adjustment turret. However, the total capacity of the *S&B 5-25x56 PMII* scope is 120 clicks (12 MRAD) with the sum of both directions, or ±60 clicks (±6 MRAD). It's worth noting that maybe wind drift correction wasn't the primary concern for the shooter at that time.

After traveling 3540 meters (3871 yards) along its trajectory, the projectile will be 337 meters (1106 ft or 13268") below the shooter's line of sight. To compensate for the projectile drop through the elevation adjustment turret, it would require 953 clicks (953 Up) or 95.3 MRAD, however the scope only supports a maximum of 260 clicks or 26 MRAD, as previously seen. Nevertheless, even if the scope allowed for 953 clicks, if the shooter missed counting just one click (0.1 MRAD) out of 953 resulting in a counting error of ~0.1%, he would completely miss the target's kill zone, which measures 0.093 MRAD in diameter.

To compensate for the projectile drop through the shooter's line of sight, it would be necessary to position the reticle's center 95.3 MRAD above the target. Thus, even at the minimum magnification (5x), which offers a 25 MRAD range for holdover, the shooter would still be unable to see his target at the moment of the shot. For the record, the projectile reaches its highest elevation at 550 meters (601 yards) along its trajectory, rising 278 centimeters or 2.78 meters (9.12 ft) above the shooter's line of sight.

Range	Time	Path	Up|Dn	Lt|Rt	Vel	Energy
m	ms	cm	Click	Click	m/s	joule
550	729	278	50D	7R	654	9834

HIGHEST ELEVATION WITH ZERO SET TO 1000M

▸ HYPOTHESIS OF ZEROING SET TO 2500 METERS

For the first hypothesis, let's consider the far zeroing of the sight set to 2500 meters or 2734 yards. Here's the ballistic table record obtained with the ballistic calculator.

Range m	Time ms	Path m	Up|Dn Click	Lt|Rt Click	Vel m/s	Energy joule
2	3	0.0↑	0	0	869	17350
2500	5K9	0.0↓	0	51R	270	1669
3540	10K	-195↓	551U	73R	224	1149

BALLISTIC TABLE RECORD WITH ZERO SET TO 2500 METERS

When setting the far zero at 2500 meters, the near zero occurs at 2 meters (2 yards) along the projectile's trajectory. We can observe that the projectile took 10 seconds (10k ms) to reach the target, with a kinetic energy of 1149 joules (847 ft.lb).

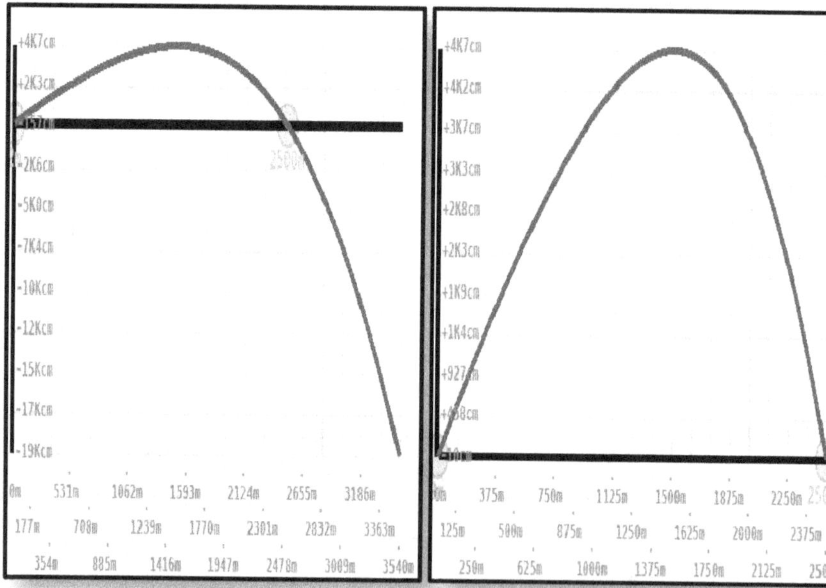

BALLISTIC CURVE WITH ZERO SET TO 2500 METERS

Considering the anticipated crosswind for the given context, it would require 73 clicks (7.3 MRAD) in one direction on the windage adjustment turret. However, the total capacity of the *S&B 5-25x56 PMII* scope is 120 clicks (12 MRAD) with the sum of both directions, or ±60 clicks (±6 MRAD). It's worth noting that maybe wind drift correction wasn't the primary concern for the shooter at that time.

After traveling 3540 meters (3871 yards) along its trajectory, the projectile will be 195 meters (640 ft or 7677") below the shooter's line of sight. To compensate for the projectile drop through the elevation adjustment turret, it would require 551 clicks (551 Up) or 55.1 MRAD, however the scope only supports a maximum of 260 clicks or 26 MRAD, as previously seen. Nevertheless, even if the scope allowed for 551 clicks, if the shooter missed counting just one click (0.1 MRAD) out of 551 resulting in a counting error of ~0.2%, he would completely miss the target's kill zone, which measures 0.093 MRAD in diameter.

To compensate for the projectile drop through the shooter's line of sight, it would be necessary to position the reticle's center 55.1 MRAD above the target. Thus, even at the minimum magnification (5x), which offers a 25 MRAD range for holdover, the shooter would still be unable to see his target at the moment of the shot. For the record, the projectile reaches its highest elevation at 1497 meters (1637 yards) along its trajectory, rising 47 meters or 4700 centimeters (1850 ft) above the shooter's line of sight.

Range	Time	Path	Up|Dn	Lt|Rt	Vel	Energy
m	ms	m	Click	Click	m/s	joule
1497	2K7	47	312D	26R	377	3263

HIGHEST ELEVATION WITH ZERO SET TO 2500M

▸ THE SHOT

Regardless of the method used to compensate for the projectile drop or the method applied for the shooter's line of sight, whether directly or indirectly, through a reference point, or even with the assistance of undisclosed tools, the bullet trajectory for this elaborated context follows as illustrated below.

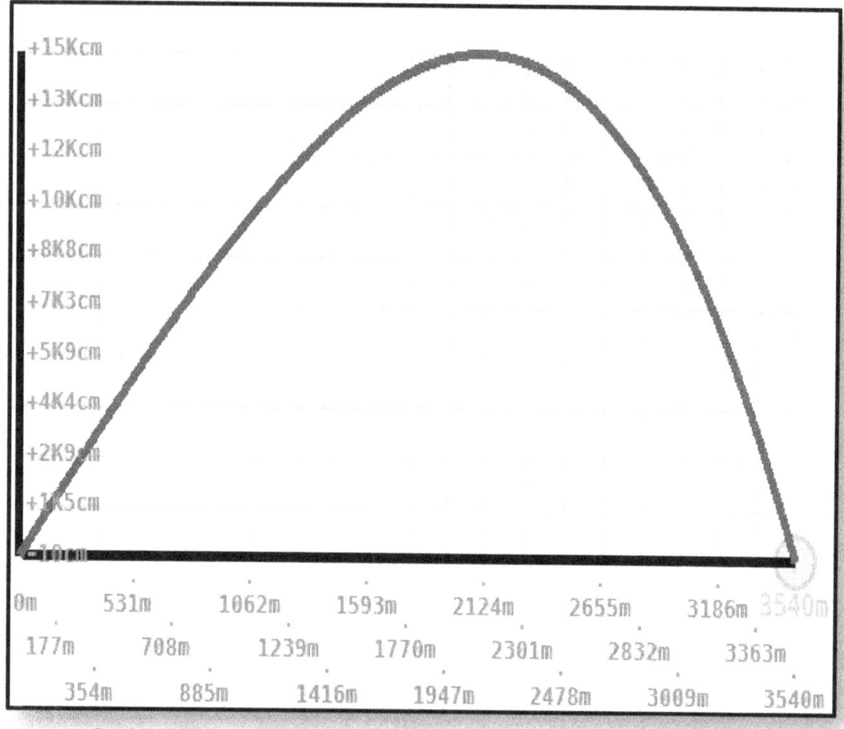

BALLISTIC CURVE OF 2017 RECORD BREAKER SHOT

| Range | Time | Path | Up|Dn | Lt|Rt | Vel | Energy |
m	ms	m	Click	Click	m/s	joule
3540	10K	0↓	0	73R	223	1139

BALLISTIC TABLE ENTRY FOR THE POI AT 3540 METERS

THE SHOT

We observe that the projectile took 10 seconds (10k ms) to reach the target, with a kinetic energy of 1139 joules (840 ft.lb), and had a velocity of 223 m/s (732 fps), which falls within the subsonic speed range. Therefore, we can conclude that the projectile passed through the transonic region, which occurs when its velocity drops to a range of approximately ±20% of the speed of sound, around 351 m/s or 1152 fps in this context. This transitional phase can lead to significant destabilization of the projectile in flight due to sudden pressure variations on its body, among other factors.

Below is an accurately scaled illustration of the 1.71 meters (~5'7") tall target and his kill zone, precisely 3540 meters (3871 yd) away from the muzzle of the Canadian sniper rifle, overlaid by the center of the *Mil-Dot Gen II XR* FFP reticle at 25x magnification of the *S&B 5-25x56 PMII* telescopic sight.

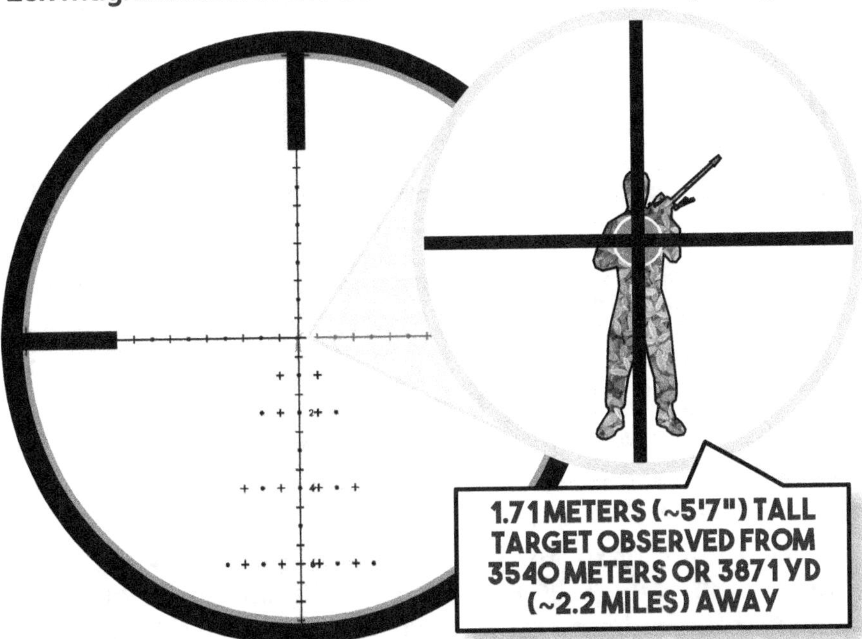

SIGHT PICTURE OF THE TARGET AT 3540 METERS AWAY, 25X

The projectile reaches its highest elevation at 2098 meters (2294 yards) along its trajectory to the target, rising 147 meters or 482 ft above the shooter's line of sight.

Range m	Time ms	Path m	Up|Dn Click	Lt|Rt Click	Vel m/s	Energy joule
2098	4K5	147	700D	41R	297	2028

HIGHEST ELEVATION FOR THE POI AT 3540 METERS

Below is a proportional illustration of the highest elevation reached by the projectile in flight and the Statue of Liberty overlaid, which has a total height of 93 meters or 305'1".

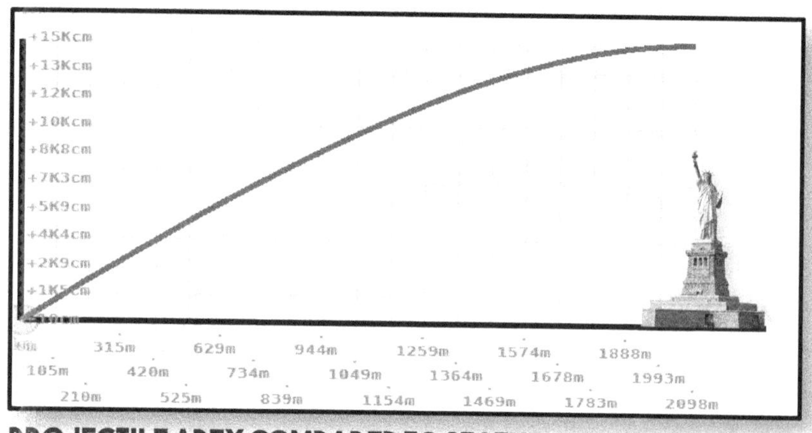

PROJECTILE APEX COMPARED TO STATUE OF LIBERTY HEIGHT

Another relevant situation to address is the accuracy applied in measuring the distance to the target at that time. Due to the considerable distance, the projectile might approach the target with a significant amount of declination. Therefore, the point of impact (POI) on the target would have occurred at a noticeable downward angle, which differs greatly from traditional representations depicting an ordinary target being hit perpendicularly in the center of its kill zone.

EXPOSING THE JTF2 SNIPER RECORD
THE SHOT

With the prominent projectile descent angle towards the target, even a 1% distance measurement error would mean a mission failure. For the 3540-meter distance, a 1% measurement error equals 35.4 meters. The ballistic table below indicates the necessary adjustments for the elevation turret if the target were offset ±35 meters from the originally perceived correct distance.

Range m	Time ms	Up|Dn Click	Lt|Rt Click	Vel m/s	Energy joule
3505	10K	22D	72R	224	1151
3540	10K	0	73R	223	1139
3575	10K	22U	73R	222	1127

BALLISTIC TABLE RECORDS INDICATING ±35 M TARGET DISTANCE

Thus, a 1% distance measurement error requires a correction of 22 clicks because it results in an elevation error of 2.2 MRAD, nearly equivalent to the height of 3 floors. Yet, even a 1-meter distance measurement error could still miss the kill zone.

Range m	Time ms	Up|Dn Click	Lt|Rt Click	Vel m/s	Energy joule
3539	10K	1D	73R	223	1139
3540	10K	0	73R	223	1139
3541	10K	1U	73R	223	1139

BALLISTIC TABLE RECORDS INDICATING ±1M TARGET DISTANCE

As illustrated above, a 1-meter distance measurement error requires a correction of 1 click, it means a 0.1 MRAD error occurrence, which is greater than the target's kill zone diameter (0.093 MRAD).

Considering the anticipated crosswind for the given context, as noted in the ballistic table for the point of impact at 3540 meters, it would necessitate 73 clicks of 0.1 MRAD, or 7.3 MRAD in one direction, on the windage adjustment turret. The *S&B 5-25x56 PMII* scope has a total capacity of 120 clicks (12 MRAD) for both directions, or ±60 clicks (±6 MRAD). However, the *Mil-Dot Gen II XR* reticle enables the shooter to compensate for crosswinds up to 5 MRAD, with hash marks every 0.5 MRAD. Therefore, the shooter could have employed both methods, dialing and holding, to apply the required correction for the wind drift.

To enhance comprehension of this essential adjustment for wind drift (WD), let us calculate, in linear measurements, the magnitude of 7.3 MRAD at a distance of 3540 meters or 3871 yards.

$$\mathbf{WD}_{METERS} = \mathbf{WD}_{MRAD} \times \mathbf{DISTANCE}_{METERS} \div 1000$$

$$\mathbf{WD}_{METERS} = 7.3 \times 3540 \div 1000 = \mathbf{25.84\ METERS}$$

or

$$\mathbf{WD}_{YARDS} = \mathbf{WD}_{MRAD} \times \mathbf{DISTANCE}_{YARDS} \div 1000$$

$$\mathbf{WD}_{YARDS} = 7.3 \times 3871 \div 1000 = \mathbf{28.26\ YARDS}$$

The wind intensity used for ballistic calculations is set to the average daytime value for Mosul at the time of the event under analysis, 15 km/h (9 mph). Note that winds up to 20 km/h (12 mph) are categorized as light winds. At the moment, we are not considering the worst-case scenarios with higher wind intensities, as is effectively the case in that region. However, even with the light crosswind considered for ballistics calculations regarding the 2017 event, it would necessitate a wind drift compensation equivalent to the length of 2 large school buses lined up.

EXPOSING THE JTF2 SNIPER RECORD
THE SHOT

Wind is an environmental factor with a high-rate of unpredictable nuances, capable of affecting the accuracy of shots. The greater the distance to the target, the greater the need for correction of the projectile's trajectory due to the wind effects; however, the greater the difficulty and imprecision in measuring this magnitude. The wind measurement at the shooter's firing position is, technically, a small and inconsistent sample of the actual wind to be faced by the projectile in its long travel to the target.

Even if the shooter waited for the perfect moment with no wind to take the shot, it would still be possible for the unpredictability of the wind to affect the trajectory of the projectile during its long flight lasting 10+ seconds.

After the shooter effectively adjusted his equipment to engage the intended target, even before pulling the trigger, we can consider that his rifle, sight, and ammunition were then set for a field-adjusted far zero (compensating for bullet drop) at exactly 3540 meters or 3871 yards.

Using the ballistic calculator, as seen below, we have confirmed that the near zero occurred within the first meter (1 yard) of the projectile's travel to the target.

```
Zero Angle.................... 5.9590 deg
Zero Ranges................... - m | 3540 m
```

ZEROS OBTAINED THROUGH THE BALLISTIC CALCULATOR

With a prominent and necessary angle between the rifle barrel and the scope to achieve the far zero at 3540 meters (zero angle or barrel angle), it is likely that the aiming device does not have sufficient mechanical adjustment range for this setting by itself.

We can convert the zero angle of 5.9590 degrees, obtained through the ballistic calculator, to MRAD, the standard angular unit used for the reticle and adjustment turrets of the aiming device used by the Canadian shooter.

$$MRAD = DEGREES \times 17.45$$
$$MRAD = 5.9590 \times 17.45 = 104\ MRAD$$

and

$$CLICKS = MRAD \div CLICKVALUE$$
$$CLICKS = 104 \div 0.1 = 1040\ CLICKS$$

Therefore, achieving an absolute adjustment of the rifle-mounted aiming device to compensate for the projectile's trajectory would require 1040 clicks (1040 Up). However, the *S&B 5-25x56 PMII* scope has an elevation adjustment range limited to 260 clicks or 26 MRAD, as mentioned earlier. Nonetheless, it's possible to indirectly achieve the necessary angle for the far zero by tilting the aiming device itself, eliminating the initial parallelism between the sight device and the firearm barrel. There are specialized devices available in the market, such as angular adjustable Picatinny/Weaver rail adapters and mounts for telescopic sights, designed for precise adjustments in elevation and/or windage, which tilt the aiming device in relation to the firearm barrel.

ANGULAR ADJUSTABLE PICATINNY RAIL AND SCOPE MOUNT

Once we know the click limits for the elevation adjustment turret and the angular limits of the markings on the vertical axis of the reticle of the aiming device used, from minimum to maximum magnification, we can infer alternatives to obtain the barrel angle of the accurate shot, which we consider to be a fact that occurred in 2017.

To achieve a steep angle between the gun barrel and the telescopic sight, we can consider the possibility of using scope mounts that provide the required tilt. Furthermore, these mounts should have significant elevation to ensure that the gun barrel does not obstruct the shooter's line of sight. A significant adjustment of the cheek rest elevation is also required, allowing the shooter to perform the shot with proper positioning and rifle stabilization.

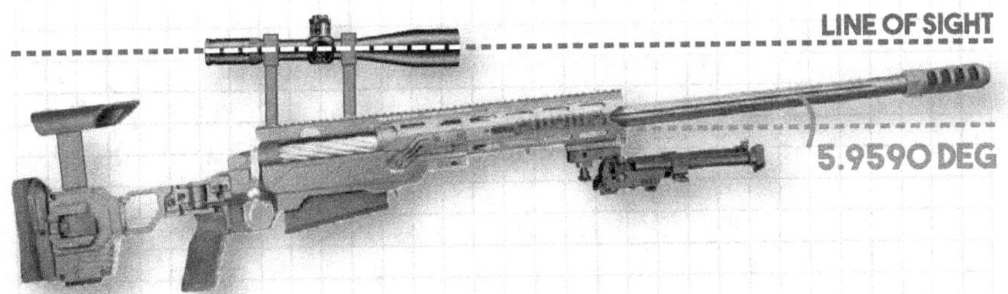

MCMILLAN TAC-50-C ANTI-MATERIAL RIFLE, 50 BMG CALIBER, S&B 5-25×56 PMII SCOPE, WITH HYPOTHETICAL ELEVATED MOUNTS AND BARREL ANGLE SET AT 5.9590 DEGREES, ACCURATELY SCALED

While possible, this mounting hypothesis for the scope presents significant challenges due to the extensive customization required for the height of each mount and the difficult installation process onto the aiming device and/or the Picatinny rail of the weapon. This is because mounting the supports on the rifle's Picatinny rail requires the same angle of inclination as that between the shooter's line of sight and the gun barrel.

EXPOSING THE JTF2 SNIPER RECORD
THE SHOT

Instead of using elevated scope mounts, the shooter might opt for a custom-made Picatinny rail adapter for elevation and angulation. Similar to the previously illustrated scope mounts, the Picatinny rail adapter must have the necessary tilt angle and sufficient elevation to avoid obstructing the shooter's line of sight by the rifle barrel. Below is an accurately scaled illustration of the hypothetical Picatinny rail adapter and the equally necessary custom elevation adjustment of the cheek rest.

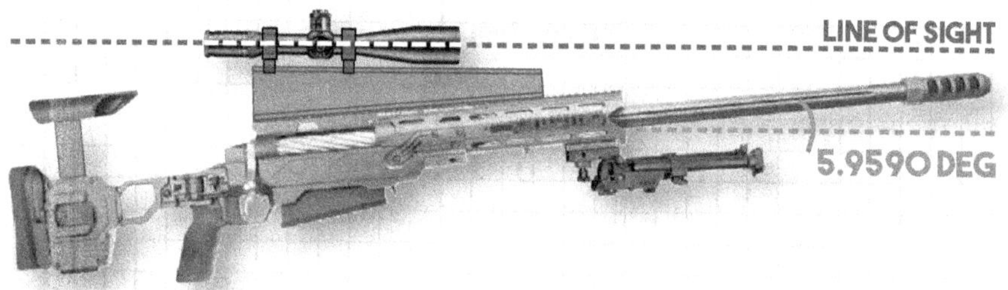

MCMILLAN TAC-50-C ANTI-MATERIAL RIFLE, 50 BMG CALIBER, S&B 5-25×56 PMII SCOPE, WITH HYPOTHETICAL PICATINNY ADAPTER AND BARREL ANGLE SET AT 5.9590 DEGREES, ACCURATELY SCALED

This type of custom-made Picatinny rail adapter for elevation and angulation was employed in September 2022 by the *Nomad Rifleman* company to achieve the self-proclaimed long-distance shooting world record. This company offers long-range shooting experiences for long-rage shooting enthusiasts.

The *Nomad Rifleman* record for the longest distance shot was not achieved in combat situations but in a controlled environment. It took 2 years and 1500 hours of work for preparation, planning, importing custom parts, reworking pieces, customizing cartridges by ammunition industries, assembly, and testing, to achieve the record of 4.4 miles, 7744 yards, or 7081 meters, but only after <u>69 attempts</u>.

EXPOSING THE JTF2 SNIPER RECORD
THE SHOT

The bullseye had a diameter of 8 inches or 20 centimeters. The target's total size was 3 meters wide and over 2 meters high, with a slope convenient for the angle of the falling bullet. The customized rifle was chambered in 416 Barrett caliber with a twist rate of 1:9. The firing system used was the same as that employed by the Canadian shooter in 2017, originally from the AMR *McMillan TAC-50 rifle*.

The Picatinny rail adapter mentioned was tailor-made to perform shots at a predetermined distance. Naturally, the customized setup by the *Nomad Rifleman* team can perform shots at different distances, although with significant limitations. Below is an image of the rifle used for the mentioned shot in 2022.

PRECISION RIFLE CUSTOMIZED BY NOMAD RIFLEMAN COMPANY 416 BARRETT CALIBER AND VORTEX RAZOR HD 6–35X56 GEN III

The aiming device used was the *Vortex Razor HD 6-36x56 Gen III*, featuring an *EBR-7D* FFP reticle and adjustment turrets with a click value of ¼ MOA. This telescopic sight was mounted on the aforementioned custom-made Picatinny rail adapter, with a 350 MOA angle.

VORTEX RAZOR HD 6–35X56 FFP GEN III TELESCOPIC SIGHT

EXPOSING THE JTF2 SNIPER RECORD
THE SHOT

The *EBR-7D* FFP reticle of the *Vortex Razor HD 6-36x56 Gen III* aiming device is mounted in the first focal plane, and its full hash marks (FHM) have intervals in 1 MOA steps. Below is an image of the reticle of the telescopic sight used for the shots made by the *Nomad Rifleman* team in 2022.

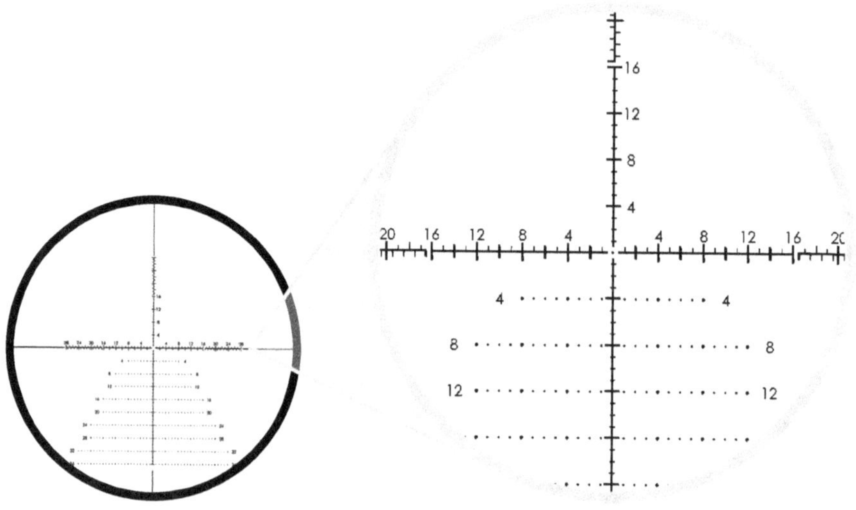

EBR−7D FFP MOA PATTERN RETICLE

For the scenario of the Canadian sniper's single accurate shot in 2017, he eventually had access to a Picatinny rail adapter, similar to the one used by the *Nomad Rifleman* company, with sufficient elevation and angle of inclination. This accessory should be attached between the rifle and the aiming device, but only for shooting at extreme long ranges. Afterward, the accessory should be removed, and the aiming device repositioned to prepare for regular long-range shots. However, precision shooters usually do not remove and reattach the telescopic sight from their rifles without going through the subsequent fine-tuning process of zeroing the sight, where even a single click adjustment requirement can compromise a precision shot.

EXPOSING THE JTF2 SNIPER RECORD
REQUIREMENTS MET FOR SUCCESS

▸ REQUIREMENTS MET FOR SUCCESS

Regardless of whether the Canadian shooter used a rail adapter to provide proper angulation and elevation of the aiming device for the record-breaking shot, it is most likely that his spotter guided his point of aim (POA) to fire against a high reference point for the resulting point of impact (POI) to occur as it did. There are other fundamental aspects that the shooter supposedly took into account to succeed in his acclaimed shot of extreme long distance and unparalleled precision in a combat context that occurred in May 2017. We will point out some.

▪ We know that the shooter was at an elevated point; therefore, we must believe that he was able to compensate for the elevation difference, as with the significant downward angle of the projectile to hit the target, due to the long distance, calculating and compensating for the inclined shot become inevitable for accuracy.

▪ The shooter accurately compensated for the inevitable spin-drift, resulting from the spin for gyroscopic stabilization of the projectile, which is sensitive for shots against targets at greater distances.

▪ Physical phenomena such as yaw, gyroscopic precession, and nutation were previously studied and included in the ballistic coefficient (BC) used for the ballistic calculations that preceded the shot.

▪ Although the supersonic projectile reached the target at subsonic speed, we can believe that there was no instability in its trajectory during its passage through the transonic region, even with the significant pressure variations that occurred in its body at this stage.

EXPOSING THE JTF2 SNIPER RECORD
REQUIREMENTS MET FOR SUCCESS

■ Atmospheric refraction, common for the city of Mosul due to its hot and dry weather, did not occur at the time of the shot, as it is capable of causing optical distortions that lead individuals (sniper and his spotter, in this case) to believe that a distant object is at a different elevation and/or distance from reality.

■ The shooter managed to measure the different wind speeds: tailwind, headwind, upward wind, and downward wind, as well as all their sudden and non-sudden changes during the projectile's trajectory, even before making his precise single shot.

■ He accurately compensated for the aerodynamic jump, capable of vertically displacing the point of impact due to the combination of crosswind and gyroscopic stabilization spin, explained by the Magnus Effect.

■ He adjusted the projectile's trajectory for its deflection due to the Earth's rotation, explained by the Coriolis Effect.

■ The Canadian sniper compensated for the parallax error of the reticle superimposed on the target, even though the last integer value indexable on the parallax adjustment scale of his scope was set to 1000 meters.

■ He did not make a mistake in measuring the distance, not even by 1 meter or 1 yard, as this would result in a point of impact displacement greater than the target's kill zone diameter.

■ The target, sniper from the Islamic terrorist group ISIS, was not effectively ready for combat and was standing and exposed, allowing the tiny 0.093 MRAD kill zone to be targeted perpendicularly.

REQUIREMENTS MET FOR SUCCESS

- The shooter either did not need to (static target) or was able to compensate for any eventual target deflection because the projectile took 10 seconds to reach the intended point of impact.

- With unparalleled skill, the shooter was able to keep the weapon stable, not allowing movements greater than 0.0465 MRAD (KZ/2) or 0.002664 degrees of angle in any direction, even with manual trigger operation, the shooter's physiology, trigger mechanical system, firing pin release, and launch.

- Finally, even after all considerations made by the shooter and his spotter, there is still the intrinsic error in the weapon's precision of 0.145 MRAD, promised ammunition precision of 0.494 MRAD but only up to 1000 meters, and scope precision for parallax adjustment with the last integer value indexable at 1000 meters and the click value for the windage and elevation turrets at 0.10 MRAD; always relating all these technical specifications to the target's 0.093 MRAD kill zone at 3540 meters away from the shooter. ~~It was luck.~~

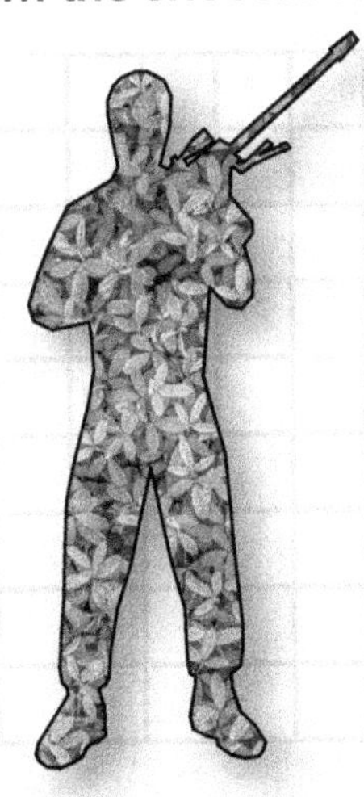

"WHOM HAVE I IN HEAVEN BUT YOU? AND EARTH HAS NOTHING I DESIRE BESIDES YOU."

- PSALM 73:25